PRAISE FOR *FOUNDLING*

"In P. R. Anderson's stoic vision, our huma[n] complex – to realize each moment in its ful[l,] pitted against the relentless drive of the universe to simplify. Into the darkness at the far rim of consciousness the poet stubbornly probes in quest of the words that will incarnate our experience. *Foundling's Island* is an impressive collection, the work of a thoughtful, assured poet undaunted by the task that awaits him."

– J.M. Coetzee

"P. R. Anderson's *Foundling's Island* is a fiercely intelligent and deeply moving collection of poems. In many ways it is the best new South African poetry I have encountered in the last decade... One feels many influences on Anderson's style, from the Classical elegy to Khoi mythology, from the Romantics to Auden, but these rich traditions never overwhelm Anderson's assured and inimitable voice: on the contrary, they serve and animate it."

– Daniel Roux, *English Academy Review*

"Careful wordplay is characteristic of Anderson, whose poems have a crystalline compression where maximum meaning is built into the fewest possible words. They are formally tight and often allusive, referring to classical models such as Horace's odes or Propertius's elegies; Anderson even essays a villanelle. But the poems themselves are not unnecessarily tricky. Several find themselves in foreign landscapes, particularly Italy, while others focus on human interactions with a wry sense of frailty but also abundance. They celebrate friendship, love, discourse and memory."

– Shaun de Waal, *Mail & Guardian*

"A poet's poet."

– Fiona Zerbst, *Sunday Independent*

FOUNDLING'S ISLAND

FOUNDLING'S ISLAND

POEMS BY

P. R. ANDERSON

UHLANGA

2018

First published by the Centre for Creative Writing, University of Cape Town,
and Electric Book Works in 2007

This edition published in Cape Town, South Africa by uHlanga in 2018

UHLANGAPRESS.CO.ZA

Distributed outside South Africa by the African Books Collective

AFRICANBOOKSCOLLECTIVE.COM

ISBN: 978-0-620-81225-2

Edited by Stephen Watson
This edition proofread by Nick Mulgrew

Cover design and typesetting by Nick Mulgrew

The body text of this book is set in Garamond Premier Pro 11PT on 15PT

To P. L. A. and E. D. A.

CONTENTS

— , for your amusement, while the rain
blows street to street and frogs begin
among your treetops, this history happens
between your gaze and recollection, pretty
much as weather marches in or wells
collect and blister. Draw up your sheets
like clouds; let the front fall – nothing
you can do will put the water back
or dry the washing now, and blessing knows
not division or degree. It rains: it pours.

VONDELINGSEILAND

At Tzaarsbank the whole Atlantic's roiling.
The coast, exposed and quarried out by water,
fronts the west as unanswerably resolute
as a martyr. Even the gulls pray.

The dunes are fossil; in their white barrows,
dreaming of violence, are the bones of legend:
sabre-toothed cats, four-tusked elephants.
They are nothing blest, but dunes that roar.

We walk a little way, cowed by wind and the lack
that is the waves' lacking intention.
The wrack is woven in a fine grain, stained
Phoenician blue, a hem of mussel shell.

Across the water the smoke of water becomes
the smoke of birds trailing from Vondelingseiland.
The rocks are furred with birds, like tripe,
the white, nitrogenous granite of a guano island.

Buildings, slipway, gantry disappear there,
but are no more derelict than a skeleton is in itself.
Perhaps boats come with booted men.
It is a nightmare but we could live there.

The stillness in the car is huge and warm,
your cigarette like our first hearth. We find
the way through the dunes is the way of the flesh.
I keep translating. Foundling's Island.

Full Moon and Porcupine

I slept on the ground in the lee of midden dunes
where the scrub was laden with mice and darker by day
than by starlight. The ocean was falling apart
on the west coast: in abraded water the moon
dissolved like a Disprin so that I slept in salts
of silver, was myself emulsified in light.

I slept and I dreamed and dreaming looked on the light.
This poem is about the interruption of light.
Sun, moon, stars – you cannot now tell them from the light
they have become, and because the light is telling.
But this is not about the light *by which* you see;
it is about the light you see, the light looked on.

I dreamed the light (that is to say I saw the fool's
light thrown in the cave of my head, foreshadowing).
But then the quick breath of a dog blew down my ear
and the light out, and the dream out – animal breath
foraging the dark for the riddle of light there
buried in my bone on the old sand full of bones.

I was hauled awake, aground under the stars' dune,
moonlight like blown sand, salt vapour high overhead,
to turn in horror from a beast that came to me
in Afrikaans out of the night – *maanhaarjakkals* –
loping towards my dream on purpose down the coast,
point-to-point from each wrecked gull and dogfish, to me.

But the light was wrong to see by, for what I saw
was light itself, as the very hackles of light
raised over me, and I could feel the light intent
upon my own skin, bristling there like crabs in sedge.
It was looking on samphire in a level wind,
saltmarsh filling, brush burning, the morse of fireflies.

I looked on the light and what I saw really was
a porcupine, close as breathing, close as a mate
at my neck, with the full moon in its eye, the stars
combed out in its quills, shaken out like a day's sand:
night's peacock, pharaoh's rat, an older god got up
in skirts of papyrus, the pig argus, the dream.

Was this what fanned the fire, fire that threw the shadow
that shadowed the bones of light, that lit the dream? They say,
you will find a porcupine wherever stars fall.
I found just this: a curious spined pig, somehow
farrowed in meteors, delivered in crashed stars,
the Beast of Transfiguration, the visitor

of dreams I was no longer dreaming. I lay out
on bone-dust strewn under a burst moon, to watch it
vanish like a sentence in its own discovery –
just like that. I woke to write it down. Morning shook
flocks of terns like snow in a Christmas toy. I saw
them, and that I saw the light – as in the night I had.

MIMOSA

Scent of itself,
intransitive,
evoking not
anything but

what it might be
being transient,
sense without sense.
It reminds me.

The years are passed.
We cast our dust
over blossom,
dust on gold-dust.

Mimosa gilds
gulley and brake,
the gates of farms,
the names of gates.

Out of the earth
sweetness and thorns,
but jealous thorns
can't pin it down.

Grace that is hard
to grasp might mean
this evasive
coming going:

yearning begun
finished, sung, grief
hoarded, heart wrung.
All sweet. All one.

LAST THINGS

It was the shore with the boats drawn up on
the last day of the world. There wasn't time
for anything but larking and they did
their hearts out. The birds were publishing it
like what was once called news. Another way
was happening and another grammar
with it and for keeps. They (sweetly laughing)
troubled with the verbs, which is, or was, to
say that they skipped stones on the falling sea:
how fast they conjugated and how brief
their stay. The tides had been withdrawn, and 'then'
not been renewed, but things were very real
like each and other, and the sand sinking,
and the sinking feeling (sweetly laughing).

AN ELECTRIC SHOCK

A small ray flying in the shallows,
the substance of its own shadow making
headway against the run of light:
creature of the realm of unlikelihood,
image of its unintelligible self
entirely, passage of pure form.

We're knee-deep in this alphabet soup.
Wading forward we turn the idea away,
it skates under pavements of crashed light.
We're left with the telling of it in the realm
of likeness, landing a haul of metaphor:
fish upon fish out of water.

Dark merman, water-drongo,
we took an oil rag for a glove puppet,
opened you like a book underwater, or
(madder still) a broker's umbrella,
but paid for conjuring your black silk
in the realm of likeness – I knew your form

for your cousin also, a lozenge of volts
laid in the sand, and the fear of it
wrapped me as precisely, substantially
as the shadow you swam into mind.
And I was shocked. I was shocked
by a skate where it lay in the sand

where the light fell, and it felt just like
light shattered in me sharply, but
not at all as I had imagined. The shock
tugged me like a drill. What appalled
was not the bond at contact, like love,
but panic – the need of words, and none.

DEMETER'S PEOPLE

Against the far dark of the late
afternoon down on 'Triangle'
a rig is mowing in the wheat

elected by sun, billowing
dust and chaff, insects, local war.
A fiery-cloudy pillar.

Over punk earth the crows come
for the parts of those mice mown
in their invisible thousands.

They've thrived as we have on this grass
found out at Jericho and like
ourselves elaborated there.

Nothing but machine and crows
waging the war of a corn god
so distant there is no report of it.

We see against darkness the sparks
fly upward, born into trouble.
The war is silent with its dead.

The lights are false, cinder-seeming
columns of units of chaff. All
travel into the farther dark

and do not scurry into stars.
We have made our world simple –
simple by wheat and with stories.

All that elaborates us
simplifies the world to one end.
What is simple is that we die;

it is not that the world should too.
The dead are Demeter's people,
cropped, and the world is simplified.

SUNDAY NIGHT

To JCA

Dusk! one says and with distaste, drawing
curtains against it, and a cork. In other
streets and other houses, more briny lights.
Separately, eggs are boiled and Mondays tidied.
Wind in the roof-iron, disconsolate, bullying.
Phonelines whimper, lamps flinch. Outside
some cricket nags like grit. There is nothing
for it, but to sleep it off and, falling
asleep, bracket the heart with others'
anguish, moving without glory just under all
that which is utterly: folding the ironing, putting
out the cat, dropping the eyes on remembrance,
turning aside, as if beheld in the theatre of rooms
in anyone's mind's eye, where the light's too wan
to operate by, the glass drained, then the light put out.

PASSAGES

As driving down both hours and provinces are traversed,
still at each passage the eyes are fetched of strangers,
glances that might be roughly history, being in each
instance the casual witness upon which we rely
for faith in the fact of ourselves, if not exactly for love,
yet the passing glance is always closed, enveloped in departure,
otherwise otherness, the prospect of war or some slow
domestic–genetic disruption, daughters at love
in the high units of cities, ecstatic, anonymous,
scarcely awake through their unemployed afternoons
flooded with the light of photographs, which is perhaps
the light of a stayed glance, in which the seen dissolves.

FRANSCHHOEK

They planted vineyards in their exile,
a new *massif central* of sorts, an end,
and bruised the mouths of others: kissing-numb
after the fruit, in the shining, old men
cycling home to their radios and their graves,
their wives and daughters brought to the dawn
in tractor trailers, the circus of the days
on the move again, the tent struck, and us struck dumb.
And this remains the massive centre of us. Now
and stooping in the white light among vines
under the wind, the mountains fold on our
hearts and the blue is on us, and our signs
suddenly become us, like a patois,
a southern wine showing the blood in its bloodlines.

Notes on a Visit to the Grave of Nongqawuse

I

Because there is that nun in us, so heart-
broken for God or the adored world,
the light's witness, we share the same confused
desire and all its consequences,
are equally cloistered, turning our hurt
out of heart, are brought to shallow graves
by history – to learn there is only a snake
between laughter and slaughter, and all
our dreams, though wonderful, are private.
Because of *because*, as every child knows,
her grave is ours, just as these lines are
now yours that were mine and will always be.

II

River after river delivered,
each silt bloom turbid with sharks
out of the blue. Small wars, broken droughts.
Flayed limbs of cactus crucified in the waves.

Dust combusts beneath us blue and bitter
all along the ridge. Country of cattle, buzzards.
Blunt wind bowing the green downs down
to the dunes they were, the sand once sea.

Bearing what has been borne this far,
the heart's cockle, badge of a kept promise,
have come at last to the red avenue
under the hill at Greenwood where

the road begins to end in the red trees there
and the farmer's found, who couldn't care,
butchering a cow, whose red hand, near,
carves directions in the air.

III

Rather blame their always being alone,
seers, informers, the moony girls going on
about voices: all those for whom the one
sustaining effort is the telling song.
They sing for private calm, to keep a world
despite the sky's clay on red-letter days,
and any slaughter they compel is told
on them by gangs that rule their yesterdays.
Children all, they know all about scapegoats.
The authors hold out a busy history;
really, it's the lonely in their shallow graves
across the world. Their songs come as echoes
to sad girls, shaking their tongues to mystery.
They see the dead alive as dolphins in the waves.

GUESTS

But these are not their real names – those got lost
in circumspection, where I once travelled, though
thank God, got safely back. What use are they?
Long after any marriage is thoroughly dissolved
in tears or acid, or the solutions that are children,
the wedding may yet be recalled for joint delight
and on this common pillow: *who else was there?**

But these are not their real names, no, for fear
of summonses or summoning too much of them –
until they crowd us as tears crowd a face
or as rain crowds a lawn, and it's a washout,
all delight dissolved, and all that's held in
common is their absence – as guests their going
under umbrellas across, then under, that wet lawn.

———————

*Beth, philologist, and Tessa, always
in the front row. David, who sold water,
for God's sake! The pretty twins, and that other
lawyer, the one who just drank beer. Etta
in her crochet, not famous yet, and the tall
Yolande we were both quite keen on, who
was proud and loved a druglord. And ambiguous
Belinda, whom you distrusted but I liked;
her schoolfriend, Lily, who was fast with men,
the daughter of a jockey, sexy. Sainted
Luisa, from Angola, and that strange
arrangement, Lulu and De Vries, since he
was out, but she adored, and they went everywhere
together. And probably still do.

Dane – the surfer – come on! – he called himself
'the brothers', lanky, shocking hair.
Prickly Seth, who married Rachel – though
she wasn't there – he borrowed a beloved
novel and never gave it back, and – oh! –
Troll Fergus, who besieged with roses
and midnight erudition. Snakey snake-oil!
Did he find love? At least not with that strictly
brilliant blonde with the Shakespearean name –
not Jessica or Cordelia, though it ends in '-a'.
I liked her. She was dear. I did my best
to foil Fergus there. Where is she now? Where
are they all, or where is each? *Oh, God. Oh, dear.*

SOME ARBITRARY FIRE

Love the Author has put down his pen.
The plot is weeds. Some arbitrary fire
kindles after the train's gone on, cinders
blow in the drains, and what comes up
is rust and glass, a crop of pain.

Fled are the surnamed valleys, long
enough for a history, with their tidy vines
and incessant river, where the train chased
over rocks like a rubble of skulls,
and Love the Author wrote it down.

Gone over the mountains, folded
like a note, where diesel magnified
the summits, the engines shook
sliding to the plateau and the milk halts where
beggars banged the train and Love was kind.

Love the Author put the miles behind –
dusk came and with it nothing – drew a blank
drawing the blind when the sun set down
on a far flat line the waste of days,
a blaze worth just a line or two.

A railyard loomed in the dining car
while the train seethed and Love looked out
on sideburned tappers whose fancied pigeons
were all now cooped asleep. Later hail
strafed the train. Love looked on flocks of sheep.

But sleep, like words, only appalled.
Love the Author, smoking through the night,
watched inky clouds spill left to right
and heard the train begin a language
proving all its points, and then tomorrow.

Love saw the light return, earth turn,
day pale in poorer suburbs where the lots ran
to weed down to the line, and there Love lost
the plot he wouldn't get, threw in his heart
with a last, fierce cigarette: into the grass.

TRAFFIC

After Propertius 4.8

After a while the days assume their idiocy
quite naturally and we can go at last
even into those uncanny places
stupid and fearless, so that the stairwell
loses its meaningful echo, the dead
leaves blow nowhere particular and your
footfall's forgotten in a new traffic.

At last. Both Teia and Phyllis are just
a cellphone away, and nobody slave
to another. They sing and I hear, they show
me their breasts and I see. Up to a point.
Taking off clothes is the first sign of tears,
but there's nobody weeps from the waist down.
Some mornings my ribs crack in the traffic.

There is no peace to be made. What I grieve
is the idiocy of days, what fools my eyes
is the hospital seen through a monkey's wedding
glittering in traffic, a port between
living and dying – as if the latter
were some sweet present continuous, like
coming, something to do with something, you.

Birds of Passage

Mudflats at mid-tide, mid-morning
reeking of nourishment, Bovril
or fish sauce, the silt puckered in
residual dimples of water,
bossed in birds' cuneiform, one vast
epic of fidgeting waders:
sandpiper, curlew, greenshank, knot,
turnstone, whimbrel, godwit, plover.
My eyes are peeled by the onshore
gusts and unblinkingly gazing
on the Field of the Cloth of Gold.

Across the water such other
pretty ducks and your famous black
eyes, starred like dark Venetian glass.
I watch through my binoculars
the low house where you lie in wait
reading your Harry Potter and
keener on breakfast than magic.
Crossing the endless boardwalk through
reedbeds that hiss, occasionally
trumpet or scream, I SMS
x's to you and they gather

in flocks ringing out low over
water: *tringa, tringa, tringa.*
Thus the thoughts of my breast arrange
in the sunlight and the sweet stench
of the quick and the dead today,
rising on purpose, that is you,
yelping down the trails towards you,
currents that ultimately sprawl
on a natal shore, as it seems by
magic, and in time for breakfast.
I break the law all the way home.

The Music

To TKL

It claimed the usual for this glade of stars
discovered in a city. As lights moved through
the dark wood, one by one, they brought their cars

to halt beneath the high horizon you
could call on fire, but was just the lit air
over Cape Town. That night a forest grew

and grew and car doors gasped like tupperware
and boots were sprung and cigarettes were kissed
goodbye on wet cement, and though despair

was in the music, it stayed there. Dismissed,
the usual yet hung on, and to the last
last song. I missed nothing and it witnessed

me, and witnessed me and you, the usual cast
asunder or together, under Mars
or Venus, watching planets as they passed.

OUR FIRST STRANGE AND FATAL INTERVIEW

Plainly: how on the first day everyone has
the same plated eyes of the bored and the lamp-
light is intermittent and submarine, and you

are still hidden like an intention, disguised
in the way I mispronounce your name, but
discovered again, as you will be in time, to time,

as the historical you. You say
only the wisest things and the wittiest, until
one day, just as your clothes become you and you

are discovered concealed by them and your eyes
take on colour: swamp, lime, copper-ash,
moss-agate, cannon-smoke, desert-rain,

then, that day, that morning, you just renounce
being various, and, focused by anger, become
not someone, but you, with the green eyes

that see it as I do, plainly, and in which I am
plainly seen and happy to be, and then
look into long enough for the green to resolve

into eyeball and outlook, the flesh and the soul.
Life is the sum of the halves of self, and seeing
that is the beginning and the end of love.

So we exchange glances, as they say, or look
into each other's eyes, in passing – this
is our treaty, before words, the licence

to halve and unite. That is the best part
and the whole of it, is it not? Perhaps
it is possible to remember it otherwise;

in fact, the first time I recall our gazes
snagging, our gazes as one gaze, was in the yard
on the last day, drinking in sunlight

under the spread hands of the chestnut leaves, our
flocked eyes combed from the fleece of talk, when I asked
who would drive me home, and you did, and stayed.

Lullaby

It's time for you and me to go to bed
protesting nothing more than hooks and eyes;
everything that needs to be's been said.

Certain the incurious stars and the dead
vigilant over us, certain and wise.
It's time for you and me to go to bed

and not to reckon damage, but instead
to tally bodies and to say just sighs.
Everything that needs to be's been said.

The suburb sleeps and doesn't look ahead
to morning and tomorrow's grieving skies:
it's time for you and me to go to bed

to grind our bones to butter and to bread
proved in the knocking and the mouth's surprise
on finding everything it needs is said

and done, and by the tongue, which being fed,
like fire or appetite, both thrives and dies.
It's time for you and me to go to bed.
Everything that needs to be's been said.

The China Plate

One sallow dusk as August palled
swiftly on hearts and summer sank
finished on cities, just as his kiss
stalled on hers, dozing in ozone
and bored to tears, two lovers rose
to a phone that sang like a frog.

There's nothing left of what was said
(all this was years ago and now
an archaeology of loss)
but it was welcome, and what's more
(or less) the matter is that all
agreed upon what happened next:

in strolling to the China Plate,
two arm-in-arm, a third in tow,
while up and down the Cowley Road
buses blew and a new air shook
raving on factories, Autumn coming
– and ardent as the baptist John –

to take their seats as the storm broke
its heart against the huge glass,
shrinking the world to there and then,
where, wrinkling in the rain, the light
on puddled paper tablecloths
sent daisies swimming in the night

like moths or stars. And they felt good
and called for drinks, lit cigarettes
and in the flame they gazed on one
another gilded by that chance
between beholder and beheld.
Consider this: they bided time.

There's nothing left of what was said
(and this was years ago, recall,
and now an archaeology)
but it was welcome, and what's more
(or less) the matter is that all
agreed upon what happened next:

a fourth came crouching through the rain,
rattling some tin bells where the door
behind him showed mercurial air
gulp like a flashbulb, and they saw
themselves dead in an instant as
enormously still as a prayer.

Something seen, something forgotten.
You had to be there, but you weren't.
There was a way of saying it, but.
Those were the days. Remember how
a duck was shred, a pancake rolled,
and on the paper written down.

But that was later, after all.
What else was said was unbegun
when, somehow struck by what had been
seen in the tin light of the storm's
door's instant's death, all four began
to talk forever and at once.

There's just this left of what was said
those years and years ago, that's now
disclosed in archaeology,
but it is treasure, and what's more
and more the matter is that all
agree upon what happened next.

It went like this: they found before
he'd wiped his glasses they were served
with *seaweed*, like an aftermath,
as if the wrack of vision, and
(though probably just greens and zeal)
they spoke in concert and in awe:

    GAMMA: Candyfloss. ALPHA: Sex.
    BETA: *Spookasem*, a ghost's breath.
    DELTA: Life itself, the green sum.
    The subjugation of Photon
    by Chloroplast in olden days.
    GAMMA: The wet lung of the world.
    BETA: Afterbirth, dowry, green
    linen. ALPHA: The knot of light.

And that is all of what was said,
now that the years have gone and gone
away and left us at a loss
again. We learn: that history is
in the occasion of the past
that's present *here*, *there*, *now* and *then*.

Casa Luisella, Licenza

To Kate Martin

Begin with a verb, it is
imperative; begin as
journeys must with a going
forward, renunciation.

So I drank all day but got
here in peace, by car and air
and bus and bus and bus and
foot, and I was almost proud.

Goodbye was business-like:
there was not nothing missing.
Passports propel as verbs do,
as queues somehow deliver.

Luisa was my forward glance –
and how she blushed at thirty
thousand feet: it was our joke,
her saying 'cabin pressure' –

but couldn't post my letters
for flying on to Paris,
not looking back. Remember.
My wine broke at Ciampino.

Voluble Italy! O
voluble heat, my bussing
without blunder, graffiti
like public hair on every

surface, plastic or pebbled,
Rome, Rebbibia, Tivoli
per CO.TRA.L and on into
the hills, the *terra santa*,

to dismount at Licenza,
my nominal objective
and termitarial Zion,
among whose nine-hundred-odd

denizens I will be known
for a week for my walking
and walking, my Diesel boots
and my surviving lightning.

In the floodplain where Horace
shifted boulders for a crop
now made over to football,
I found my lodging, and here

I came to rest with sprinklers
ticking the afternoon off,
resinous, appley wine, dusk
begotten of dogs and stars

slowly, slowly. All these things
plus the hoopoe at the ruins,
the storm, my friend Adamo,
fiori di zucca, shouts,

cars on gravel, dragonflies,
sodium lamps, Sirius,
a fall in a ditch, my feet
bleeding in water, small fish,

make an end of it. What was
began. Things are what remain;
nouns are what is left of verbs.
They are my ruins, are what was.

VILLA DI ORAZIO

To Clive Chandler

O Clive, whose vivid self
sponsors the rhyme 'alive',
more Ghibbeline than Guelph
(your nickname connotes 'throw'
but rhymes with 'fuck'), you know
to live means 'be alive'
eternally today
(I know you know), and though
the tax on it is grave
(*in vino veritas*),
vital to be no slave,
vital to be just us –
I wish that you could skive
with me into these hills'
heat and holm, and holm's shade
sweet with summer diesels
and older thunders, brave
the serpents I was warned
about, the falling tree,
and drink wine (warm) (but free)
and gravely laugh with me.

FONTE BANDUSIA

To Annarita at Al Boschetto, Licenza

Annarita, let me be candid – it
is not your food, but writing, while I eat,
my phrasebook-ransom-notes to you that makes
my day. The food's okay. It's more the way
that you inhabit nylon and your wine
tastes like a nosebleed in a swimming pool.
Your niece came up and said "Ello", then spun
away in pirouettes and giggles, and
I saw her breasts were budding as a kid
puts forth the kind of almost-horns that once
condemned one to the water where I write.
We say in English: 'He's taking licence',
and that I am: your poet's licence-to,
but you well know you live in licence here
under the hill, the spring that says 'amen'
again and again and with which (or whom)
I share these words, my wine, and being here.

Piazza della Libertà

Before I got to coffee heat was served
like notice. I walked without a shirt. There
was that menace before noon. The tables
spun like coins: I should have called the lightning
in their zinc. She came again and saw me
see her sit down spare and awkward on the wrong
side of the square. A pram redeemed her there.
I walked the other mile, the mile away
and down and stole three figs and cut my hand
in doing so, and a hooded crow or
more saw (*saw*, *saw*, *saw*) me doing so. God,
it was hot. Not wine, not water put me
out; I swallowed air. But then the day got
taken like a photograph, and thunder
shook lizards from their walls and then the rain
first smudged, then floored, the butterflies – then came.

Returning late to the lindens and laboratories of Cirey, risking
late or the camber of ice, the carriage of Émelie du Châtelet topples.
By two or three lanterns descry the chaos: horses in their traces
milling the snow as the cart comes down grating, almost elegantly,
with a tinkle of glass. In the aftermath hear the groom crooning
Steady, Steady, and the almost complicit and very polite hysteria
of those brushing the snow off each surprised other and proving
their bones and their memories. Throwing its head a horse is found
serviceable, and soon will come rescue, officious and noisy,
a party of lights and ice-amplified speech and a sled, and then soup
and bed, with a brick from the fire, and tomorrow, work.

But for now we are waiting in the far night, brittle and fricative
and far as the far-hearing ear can hear, blue under starlight
the substance of dust. It is an immense interruption.
Voltaire and the footman (who could be you) are hauling out
rugs, furs, bolsters, coats, hats, and these, and more, you set
against a drift that is sound, some way away, and there the lovers,
whose doting and whose character of thought can be felt as warmth even
now as they put out the lamp, lean back into the eiderdown of snow, are held
in common arms, that are the comfort of the ages, in a history of rime,
heads full of mathematics and Latin, and (thanks to you) a little brandy,
to look up at the stars falling into the profound west (as you do), like snow.

CADE LAMBS

The bit that troubles me
most is not appetite,
the culture of hunger,
but the emendations,
scraps of script, Linear B,
tattooed on the dry fat
in mortuary violet,
mortuary green, gentian,
cochineal pink, or
Windsor and Newton ink.

And caught looking on
lit meats, the arrangements
of trauma, as if with
belladonna pupils,
how my friend from Classics
behind his own gurney
confirms my confusion.
Some things are better left
unsaid, unseen: that we
pat the cuts, palm meat, keen.

Dusk, then, in memory
(far from the strip-lit aisles):
brisk rural dark, night wind
out of the valley, smoke
and sheep-shit, the nightjar,
cunning devices of gates,
coming upon the cade lambs
complaining, to cheat them
with our fingers for teats.
We shiver, we linger.

JUDAS GOAT

In front of death there is a goat going
over and over the bridge to the fields
where the grass is always greener, over
the troll who knows each trip for a trap.

In front of death there is a goat going
into the desert with a jaundiced eye,
lucky in lots and with a prize of sins
laid on his liberty in the world's way.

In front of death there is a kid growing
horns for a history of love or war
never to happen, but its blood will make
water famous at the hand of a poet.

In front of death there is a goat going
in practised measure, surefooted, headlong
down the ramp to the knives and sluices,
bleating for all the world like a poet.

Your Works

Afternoon palls: the dog snaps at a fly.
You should be here but for no reason, nor
is 'you' entirely clear – just as the sky
that got dragged out all week is now dragged in
to yet another argument. What for?
Tomorrow closens, but first paraffin
to light the lamps, then girls to bath, then gin.
This was where we came in and this remains
immediate and our prospect, though that 'our'
cannot be told for certain like a lie.
The thing is what is present, that and our
disclosure, like the sky, like when it rains
and 'sky' is academic, but the drains
drink and the tank is filled. Your works begin.

Talking after Dark

The days repeat themselves
and hour by windless hour
the birds' *et ceteras*
contrive philosophy:
we go about our work
blessing all even things,
and even so ourselves
we have the measure right
for talking after dark
(we sleep outside at night).

And while the world ignores
such uneventful lives,
we, pottering about
our sunlit clearing, know
the blessing vests in us
thus blissfully becalmed.
At anchor we have spread
our maps like treasure:
my great-aunt's writing board
absorbs what little pressure

our lives transmit, while there,
knee-deep in the plumbago,
lunch is laid and laughter
reminds us of our bodies'
capacity for pleasure.
This is our common ground
whose peace we have betrayed
in anger or in sorrow,
brooding on passing time,
living only for tomorrow.

Here on the eastern coast
a corrugated land
conceals us from the sly
ambition of the sea,
its whispered love and grave,
imperial embrace.
We have all history
in which to reckon bones,
and all that history shows
is mortal frontier zones.

And so we love this place
in part because it's not
yet our inheritance.
For now the flaming sword
is rumoured but deferred,
and though on evening walks
we hear the gardener
sing in his teeth and wield
his shears, and see them flash,
yet now we need not yield.

We sleep outside and dream
that ghosts file down the paths
into the colony
and each one carries fire
and knows full well how dreams
cover our days like thatch.
Stars fall but not on us.
We are in love for now
with now. The dead forgive
better than we do now.

Love tied the knot of time
in you and me and now
our knotted hearts become
the measure of our love.
This is the riddle prompts
all poetry and why
we find our selves confound
the promise they once showed
of the abundant life:
we are a twisted code.

From ridge to ridge the fires
wink to affirm our part.
There is no scheme of things.
Old wars are still being fought
in this unlikely time,
this complicated land,
and will not go away
completely or for good:
what keeps the heart in time
is ultimately blood.

What draws the infant's breath
rusts in the course of veins;
what shakes the lover's ribs
flows to the field of war.
This is what we are here for.
This is what is so sore.
'Together' calls the pulse
under stars, under sheet,
under skin, under sleep.
Together is how we meet.

This is the common life
we thought we had in mind,
braving our various fears –
the unmarked car, the phone
dissolving sleep in news,
the stranger overnight
whose disappearing first
brought panic to the door.
Our rumoured future came
closer and something more:

it came to mean our shadows
cast by the fire of war
share in a mutual dark
without distinction, share
the common future that
is all of ours, in which
we find our common cause.
We find that cause is one
because we always lose
the world we have begun,

and if our cause against
extinction cannot win,
we are constrained to make
common cause with one
world while we can, to keep
abundant the abundant
life in which we find
ourselves in love, at work
with sunlight on our backs,
or talking after dark.

THE PASSING WORLD

On and on and it becomes a state of mind, less
list than litany, the recitation of trains
terminating somewhere, always else, where lives go
on, and go on becoming lives, but first are kept
a little longer from themselves, racing across
ploughland, say, or halted in a summer cutting
or (once) alongside poplars in French snow for what
seemed an ice age. There is that freedom in arrest,
being *in parenthesis*, travelling like luggage
crammed in the couplings on a long-weekend, or held
like breath, vaulting Rannoch Moor and gazing down on
stags scattered into the bog, cantering silent
across the tar ponds, balancing antlers, their hooves
dragging in amber, ghosts, like the stars of old film.
Coming and going is our suspended sentence.
It will end (in tears) for all sentences have that
destination in the vast, loud-spoken concourse
under the station clock; all go to the thing said
in the saying. But getting there is our freedom
just as it is inevitable – thus we know
there's no good worrying about the iron left on
once the platform's gone and suburb succeeds suburb,
belonging to someone, like sadness, arbitrary.
All of that misery is neither here nor now
though tomorrow may arrive as a telegram
following us, even as we anticipate
arbitrary sadness, watching the builders' sand blow
into excavations, as we blow through, foresee

swimming-pools as nosebleeds or drownings, burned-out homes.
Where we were going was mostly where we were meant.
(Although, once, aimed for Calais I woke in Ostend
gaping at warehouses written in Afrikaans.
Flemish gendarmes took me for a spy and I got
put on a boat, then drunk, reckoned myself not yet
eighteen but on the home stretch, and was right and wrong.)
There was arriving at dawn in pecan orchards
hung in a green mist like gas, on an overnight
overrun by migrants wanting Christmas at home,
who hammered our door down with an ironing board
and paid by sharing brandy, cooped among chickens.
And not arriving: woken by frontier police,
lying wrapped with my cousin, together gilded
by sunrise in mountains above Turin, I first
saw snow and what it was: flotsam of ice and light
compounded, streaking the gravel-bed, returning
the principal of those who haven't slept, whose eyes
are hot with waking's radiance and looking on
those who did not sleep with them. It was forever
getting there that counted and the proof is I do
not much recall specifics of arrival, save
manhandling luggage through high doors and jumping down
just in time, always anonymous: there were no
lovers conjured in steam, no exile's receptions.
At Mallaig there was just time for Scottish measures
in a bar with a linoleum floor, before
taking the same train out; the kiss on the platform
was wind, cold as a sailor, a mouthful of scales.
The journey is why the junctions derive their fame
as the back of beyond, somewhere nobody wants

to go, but all must pass through. Theirs are the proper
nouns of fate. One can construe *Slough* as of despond
or *Crewe* as, thrice, the cock's laughter after the fact.
I told you so. I told you so. I told you so.
And *De Aar* sounds like clay's first uttering itself:
de aarde, the earth, but properly is *de aar* ,
the vein, is the world's vein, and which we travel.
There's nothing there but De Aar, a knot of rail, scorched
odour of creosote on sleepers that are laid
out like the dead and as numerous on the earth.
And there are night junctions, where sleep is a lurching
across passages of shunting to unmeasured
silences falling without reason: Alicedale,
where I once wept with relief to be gone from, far
into the elsewhere of the night, a place without
any other purpose but the trains, the station
burning its lights and its men barking in the cold.
Or deserting Venice, deserted on the first
night of the year, ahead of weather: that weather
overhauled us in the sidings at Padua
waiting for a connecting train, to take on troops –
I recall only how dressy they were and young
(as I was), sleeping on shoulders, and also that
they gave us tangerines, in the familiar night.
However we come to be going wherever
we are, the junctions signal junctures, they stand for
journeys that are not to and fro, but through, that go
from A to A, but not nowhere, nor returning
us to our points of departure – not exactly.
That is why the junctions are as much where we were
going as the destinations for which we seemed

to set off: the far side of our journey's moon,
consequential but irrelevant to purpose,
yet keeping an option on that purpose, being
zero-rated and therefore infinitely more
likely to surprise. We find it was at De Aar
we lost our heart or accepted Occam's Razor,
dreamed, or talked to the inevitable stranger.
Needing to go where yet we have no need to be
discovers us to ourselves like treasure; we find
that windows are also mirrors where our profiles
are coined on the passing world, spent and buried there,
and, hidden behind our eyes, become transfigured –
not decorated by light, but translated out
of this world. And so we are often sad on trains,
unwittingly mindful of what is passing on:
train, landscape, self, world, life, it can be said simply.
Because the point is no point, that instances are
without significance in themselves, like stations
brought into being by the railway, more or less
identical, we grieve ourselves and the world bound
on a journey beyond us, where all's one, and so
our sadness on trains is also sweet with yearning:
desire of ourselves and of the world, and of union
and equivalence, just as we see accomplished
through and in the window, where all prepositions
are one, and so, however they are signalled, all
sentences thus travel to the same thing said. This
is the gift of tongues, translating out of this world.
Once, headed for Jemelle, a day in the Ardennes,
we tunnelled through woodland, mile after mile, a trench
cut across Belgium, and though we were traversing

the dead thunder of American tanks, the Bulge,
still it looked like Africa – the way the bush grows
sheer to the strip-roads and soon enough everywhere
could be anywhere. It is on foot that the world
is particular: beyond Jemelle were copses
cordoned with incident tape where bait had been laid
for rabid foxes, some NATO jet shook the air
low over four countries, and there were *fraises des bois*
underfoot and a Madonna riddled with light.
That world of detail is dear to us for its forms
(a couple in rain, anoraked, walking the dogs
somewhere between London and Cambridge) because each
is unique really, though sprung from the one idea
(that is also the idea of *one*). These make us
happy the way the thought of their loss makes us sad.
But travelling dissolves detail, specific forms,
as we pass (the time) in the passage of ideas,
kept from what we think of as real lives, even though
our real lives persist on the train, suspended there
in the window, there displaying our hope of death.
If the self in the world and the self on the train
are continuous and we know it, then at least
we have clear the idea of self, knowledge of it,
and not just the fact, often awkward, of our forms
headed heaven knows where; at least we see what might
be the extent of self, what might become of us
after all. Out of the bush at a milk halt came
a woman singing in the sunrise just beyond
the bridge at Bloukrans (where long ago the train fell),
who climbed up out of the thicket of what is real,
the history of that day's aloes and birdcall,

the paths of cattle, milk cans struck with morning light,
onto the train, putting her song away that was
one part of the burden on her head, beautiful,
to fall silent there, laying her eyes on the passing
world, dissolving as detail, into what is not
a dream but the fact under dreaming. I saw her
then out of this world, who had been in it, and there
also what becomes of me, years later, standing
alongside my (now dead) grandfather in winter
dark, as the frost comes down on the ash of grassfires,
waving a torch at the coming engine, saying
goodbye quickly, while the diesel bends the stars, and
climbing into the lit carriage out of the dark
farm that then becomes nowhere and takes him with it.
It can be said simply and that is what is done.

ST PETER'S CHURCHYARD

Barren as the backyards of poverty, the whole
graveyard listing to the vivid lagoon,
the graves thus harrowed, it's just dust, dust the colour
of the ash of people, a shade darker
than dust. Pumice earth, hot, so that all the fallen
jars derive agate, the volcanic cast
of glass, wax flowers, bright funerary gravel.
The sand so scalding that the robins roll
dark on their own spheres of shadow, from shade to shade
in the rubble of these dead whose names are
the roll of days under suns or surgery lamps,
salt fogs, Atlantic fronts, the kind of slow
caustic attrition that has chewed the graves' cement
to dough: Barsby, Pedersen, Wilsnagh, Lloyd.
Now cairns are raised on this dereliction, fashioned
of what remains, much as our own selves are
aggregated dust, spacejunk, the accomplishment
of odds and ends, compounds of immense force.
The cairns are heaped on the bones of themselves, risen
out of the tombs of bad cement that lime
bound and lime dissolved, as if to scour the souls there
of the bodies' suet – sin – with ash, with lye.
But the souls are long gone into anonymity;
one by one the names fall with their headstones,
artefacts once of love, now articles of faith.
We know not what they were, nor even that.
And the graves of children remind us that a soul
is not a self, the work of a lifetime,

to be grown into like a name, inhabited,
but just the will of an idea, begotten
not made, not really ours, yet our common purpose.
It is not knowing whom you contemplate
under the piles of rusk stone, the small pyramids,
confounds. It is the facts speaking for them-
selves, soul to soul, without all personality.
Look up from the ash heap to the known world
under the lamp of your day there: that vivid blue
will draw your breath. It is so beautiful.
Across the lagoon the gantries of Saldanha
scaffold the monuments we most desire
in all the world, that sky, blue water, fishermen
trawling the shallows and the deep, the warm
dark dust of the dormitory of St Peter.

Notes

'Full Moon and Porcupine'
'For this place it really is which the porcupine is at, where the stars fall' – Dia!kwain.
W. H. I. Bleek and L. C. Lloyd, *Specimens of Bushman Folklore* (253).

'Mimosa'
'Mimosa (mod. L. app. F. L mimus MIME sb. + –osa fem. –osus suffix.) The name
seems to have been meant to allude to the 'mimicry' of conscious life shown by the
Sensitive Plant.' *Oxford English Dictionary*.
   The latter, *mimosa humilis*, is not the concrete object of the poem, but the
attributes it donates, both to the name of the genus and to the poem, share in the
purport of the poem.

'Last Things'
dulce ridentem: the sweet laughter is overheard, in Horace, *Odes*, 1, 22 (23).

'Demeter's People'
'Another trace of her tendency to become a goddess of the depths of the earth and
not simply of the corn is shown in the Athenian use of ... 'Demeter's People' as a
euphemism for the dead.' *Oxford Classical Dictionary*.

'Franschhoek'
Site of the settlement of French Huguenot refugees from the late 17th century
onwards. In invoking the *massif central* I have in mind the Protestant holdouts of
the High Cevennes and the Camisard uprising of 1702–3 (and its suppression).
The poem owes a direct debt to Thomas Pringle's sonnet of the same name.

'Notes on a Visit to the Grave of Nongqawuse'
Nongqawuse was the most prominent prophet of the Xhosa Cattle-Killing of
1856–7, a figure whose startling visions suffered the systematic manipulation of her
own patriarchal society and the scapegoating posterity of both Xhosa and colonial
histories. She is reputedly buried on a farm in the Alexandria district of the Eastern
Cape, where a (subsequent) memorial may be found in a thicket of pine trees and
tecoma, in the middle of a wide, green field.

'Traffic'
In his Elegy 4.8 Propertius recounts the hilarious and unfair revenge of his mistress
Cynthia when he affects a bachelor's recovery from her desertion – but with
little relish and less success. Teia and Phyllis are the good-time girls with whom
Propertius plans to spend an evening in Cynthia's absence. The best translation by
far is to be found in Gilbert Highet's *Poets in a Landscape*.

'Birds of Passage'

In love poetry aimed at an actual person there is always a danger that the frame of reference will prove exclusively private and inaccessible.

It was Anne Boleyn who had the black eyes and whose breasts Henry VIII described as 'pretty ducks'. In 1520 she was present at the 'Field of Cloth of Gold', the great court of Anglo–French amity.

Tringa is a genus of sandpiper; the word accurately relays the flight call of those species.

'Our First Strange and Fatal Interview'

The title is from Donne, 'Elegy', 16.

'Casa Luisella, Licenza', 'Villa di Orazio', 'Fonte Bandusia', 'Piazza della Libertà'

Four odes in an Horatian vein, written on a visit to the ruins of Horace's villa in the Sabine hills. 'Casa Luisella, Licenza' vaguely recalls Horace's journey to Brundisium (*Satires* 1:5), and directly recalls his thanksgiving for the Sabine estate ('Hoc erat in votis' ... this was in my prayers, *Satires* 2:6) 'Villa di Orazio' recalls Horace's many celebrations of friends and friendship. 'Fonte Bandusia' refers directly to the Bandusian spring made famous in *Odes* 3:13 ('O fons bandusiae...'). Licenza, the name of the village nearest to the site of Horace's villa, is derived from the Latin *Digentia*, in Horace's time the name of the river running in the valley below. The modern name is a homonym of the Italian common noun meaning 'licence', and sponsors the pun in 'Fonte Bandusia'.

'An Enlightenment History of Snow'

The anecdote of Voltaire and Du Châtelet's accident is recounted in Richard Holmes's 'Voltaire's Grin' (*Sidetracks* (2000) 353). Nancy Mitford's *Voltaire in Love* offers a fuller version, but it is Holmes's that I have in mind. Voltaire is much the better-known figure, but Du Châtelet's contribution to intellectual history is probably greater. A full account of the relationship appeared in David Bodanis's *Passionate Minds* (2006).

'Cade Lambs'

'Cade adj. Of the young of animals: cast by the mother and brought up by hand.' *Shorter Oxford English Dictionary*.

'Judas Goat'

The Judas goat is trained to lead sheep into an abbatoir. The four stanzas of the poem trace the ambiguous cultural history of goats, or rather of humankind's self-recognition in the goat. The reader will recognise references to the folktale of the Billy Goats Gruff, the Biblical account of the scapegoat in Leviticus 16:20–2, the sacrificial kid of Horace's *Odes* 3.13, and to the Judas goat itself.

'The Passing World'

Although the poem concludes with a full stop, it is serpentine in conception. Metrically, the hexameter is a syllabic derivation from (and nod towards) Lucretius's *De rerum natura*, usually translated as *On the Nature of the Universe*.

'St Peter's Churchyard'

At Churchhaven on the west coast of South Africa, a chapel in the archdeaconry of Hopefield. The word 'cemetery' shares, in its etymological history, in the sense of 'dormitory'. The metre attempts a loose English version of the metre of Latin elegy (in itself not sharing the business of threnody or memorial understood by 'elegy' in English).

POETRY FOR THE PEOPLE

— ALSO AVAILABLE —

In a Free State by P.R. Anderson

White Blight by Athena Farrokhzad, translated by Jennifer Hayashida
IN ASSOCIATION WITH ARGOS BOOKS, USA

Zikr by Saaleha Idrees Bamjee

Milk Fever by Megan Ross

Liminal by Douglas Reid Skinner

Collective Amnesia by Koleka Putuma
CITY PRESS BOOK OF THE YEAR 2017

Thungachi by Francine Simon

Modern Rasputin by Rosa Lyster

Prunings by Helen Moffett
CO-WINNER OF THE 2017 SOUTH AFRICAN
LITERARY AWARD FOR POETRY

Questions for the Sea by Stephen Symons
HONOURABLE MENTION FOR THE
2017 GLENNA LUSCHEI PRIZE FOR AFRICAN POETRY

Failing Maths and My Other Crimes by Thabo Jijana
WINNER OF THE 2016 INGRID JONKER PRIZE FOR POETRY

Matric Rage by Genna Gardini
COMMENDED FOR THE 2016 INGRID JONKER PRIZE FOR POETRY

the myth of this is that we're all in this together by Nick Mulgrew

AVAILABLE FROM GOOD BOOKSTORES IN SOUTH AFRICA *&* NAMIBIA
& FROM THE AFRICAN BOOKS COLLECTIVE ELSEWHERE

UHLANGAPRESS.CO.ZA

Printed in the United States
By Bookmasters